YOUR PICTURES CREATE YOUR LIFE

KLAUDIA S.W

DEDICATED TO PATRICK AND CHERYL

who brought happiness, joy, and smile to everyone that they came into contact with.

Both gone too early and are deeply missed.

Contents

Foreword

Acknowledgement

Introduction

Chapter 1 (What is this 'Thinking Stuff'?)

Chapter 2 (Mind)

Chapter 3 (Faith)

Chapter 4 (Gratitude)

Chapter 5 (Goals)

Chapter 6 (Visualisation)

Chapter 7 (Routine & Discipline)

Chapter 8 (Self-Image)

Chapter 9 (Thinking and Acting in The Certain Way)

Chapter 10 (How to Calm Your Mind)

Epilogue

Books for Further Reading

To Shaff,

If you knew how powerful you are, you would <u>NEVER</u> doubt yourself again!
Show the world who the FK you are!

Love,
Claudi
xxx

Foreword

April 28th, 2012, was a day I will never forget. I lived in England with my son, just us two, and we were going out to the park with my best friend Cheryl and her two beautiful daughters, Angel and Crystal. Angel was the same age as my son. They were the best "partners in crime".

Just like any other nice day, kids were playing in the park, we were chatting and moaning about life being hard and a struggle, especially both being single mums. Then, as we were walking back home, I asked Cheryl if she wanted to come over for dinner. She said, "Yes, that would be great hun."

We got home, and I turned on my laptop, telling Cheryl that my brother was going to Skype me in a minute and that she could say hello while I prepared dinner.
I waited and waited - but there was no phone call, so I decided to call his mobile. He was in Slovakia, and I had no other way to get hold of him. The phone was off, and I did not know why, as he never used to turn his phone off. So, I decided to ring my mum to find out what was going on. My mum's phone was off too.

I got a very bad feeling, and so I rang my dad. My dad's phone was ringing, but no answer. Then I went on Facebook to see if my brother was online, and that was when I found out that my brother died.

One of my friends on Facebook had put on my timeline 'So sorry for your loss. Patrick will be missed very much'.

At first, I thought it was a bad joke, but then more and more people wrote the same thing on my timeline, and I could not believe it.
I decided to contact one of my good friends, who was a police officer in town where my brother lived, and he confirmed that my brother had died. He was a close friend of my brother and could hardly speak as he told me that Patrick had been involved in a car crash. The driver survived, but his passenger, my brother, did not.

After that phone call, I passed out. Fortunately, Cheryl was there and helped me. Then Cheryl booked tickets for us to fly back home.
I remember how I hated everything and everyone, especially the boy that killed my brother.

A few weeks after I returned to the UK, I was watching WWF one night, and then it happened.
Rayback was talking about a book that has changed his life. The name of the book was "The Secret." For some reason, I became obsessed with knowing what is the book about. I started to search for it and found it. I was reading it online and fell in love with it right away.
The next day I found a movie of the book and watched it. I decided to have a hard copy of the book in my hand, so I took my son for a walk, and we went into a book shop, and it was there, right in front of me. So, I bought it.

I started to read it again and became attracted to one person that featured in the book. That person was Bob Proctor.

There was 'something' about him, and I also loved the way he spoke in the movie. I started to follow Bob and subscribed to his page. His thinking, his way of life was so amazing that I wanted my life to be as fantastic as Bob's.

I started to read books that Bob advised me to read, and **sometimes** I did what Bob suggested to do. I was going back and forth with my thinking for a couple of years. I even found a man of my dreams who I loved so much, and I still do. His name is Curtis. I attracted him into my life prior to Bob's teachings without even realising that I was using the Universal Law - as, at that time, I had no idea that there were Universal Laws.

However, things weren't great as my mind was full of mixed thoughts, and our relationship was shaken up! I knew that I had to change; otherwise, I would never live the life I wanted to live, and I would never be happy.

As I was thinking about how to change everything, I got an email from Bob inviting me to Paradigm Shift Seminar that was starting in a few days. I knew it was the only chance for me to change everything and so I bought an online stream and watched it for three days on my laptop! The person that closed the laptop after those three days was a new, completely changed girl. I finally understood how to use my mind, my thoughts, my feelings, and most importantly, I knew how to save my relationship and my life. I signed up for Bob's 13 months coaching program, and I decided to work with Bob.

I realised that I could live the life I truly desire and have, be and do everything that I want as I AM the creator of my life, just as everyone in this world is the creator of their life.

This short book will reveal to YOU how to use your mind, change your thinking, and stay positive so YOU can live the life you really want to live. It is not hard at all; in fact, it is very easy and fun.

Enjoy

Acknowledgement

I want to express my deepest gratitude to Bob Proctor and Sandy Gallagher for showing me how to live the life I truly desire. Andres Rivera Hurtado for bringing me into PGI 's program and guiding me and supporting me at all times. Pixie Low and Kathy Gallagher for their phenomenal coaching work and support and encouragement.

Peggy McColl, who put the idea of writing a book in my mind.

To my son Damian, who lights up my life every day, and to my partner Curtis Warren for all his support, patience, and love. To my parents for their never-ending love and support.

To Anthony Barraclough for sharing his phenomenal skills and knowledge with me.

To all the brilliant teachers who inspired me: Dr. Wayne Dyer, Earl Nightingale, Napoleon Hill, Genevieve Behrend, Thomas Troward, Wallace D. Wattles, James Allen, Neville Goddard, Dr. Joseph Murphy, Andrew Carnegie, Robert Kiyosaki, Warren Buffett.

A grateful heart
IS A MAGNET FOR MIRACLES

Introduction

" What you think you become "
(Buddha)

You are the creator of your own life. You are meant to live an abundant life. Not abundant only in the financial sense, but in all other areas too.
You have the right to be rich, to feel rich. Rich in health, in relationships, in your career, and financially. You are meant to do **everything** that you want to do, to go **everywhere** where you want to go and **do** and **be** whatever it is that you want to do and be.

Every morning when you wake up, you should be excited for a new day and great things ahead of you. And yes, there will be challenges in your life too, but this book will help you to overcome them and stay on track. Challenges are not bad. Thanks to them, we learn how to grow and stay persistent and have *faith*.

"I see only my objective – the obstacle must give way."
(Napoleon Bonaparte)

CHAPTER 1

What is This 'Thinking Stuff'?

*" If the average person said what they were thinking,
they would be speechless."*
(Earl Nightingale)

When I read The Secret, I did not understand what was this' thinking stuff' that the book was talking about. It took me years to find out what it is and how it works.
It was the 'Paradigm Shift Seminar' that really helped me to understand how powerful my thinking is and what it can do for me. I also became aware that this 'thinking stuff' can be very good for me, but it also can be very harmful if I don't use it to my advantage and leave it on 'autopilot.'
I knew a proverb that says *'What you think about you bring about,* 'but I didn't really grasp the true meaning of it until I started to study with Bob.
To change our lives, we must understand and become aware of our *thoughts.*
When you think about negative situations, you are creating more of the same bad things which will come to you. Then you wonder WHY you are having a bad day; a bad life. Let me tell you WHY. It is because that is what you are thinking about, and the Universe will move all circumstances for you to reflect **your** thinking. If you are thinking about something good, such as a nice situation, that is what you will attract. Nice, positive, joyful,

and happy circumstances, as that is the signal that you are sending out to the Universe.
I know from my own experience that it is much easier to think negatively than to think positively. That is human nature, but it is also the reason why 95% of the population are living a hard life and struggle every day in every area of their life.
Thinking is the hardest work to do, which is why only a few people engage in it.
Only 2% of people really **think;** 3% think they think, and 95% would rather die than **think!** (This is a proven fact as stated by George Bernard Shaw).
Thinking is one of our higher faculties that separate us from animals. Humans have sensory faculties; we can *hear, see, smell, taste, touch*. Animals also have them, but what separates us from the animals are our **higher faculties**, *memory, perception, will, imagination, intuition,* and *reason* – ***thinking!***
If you want to change your life, if you want to live a good life, you must start thinking of a good life, and you will attract it. We live in a world of thought. Thought is the only power that can produce a tangible riches.
That is the way how everything was created. It all started with a thought.
The Wright Brothers invented an airplane because they had a thought that they could create something that would take them up to the sky so that they could fly like birds do. And they did. Today, we can get from one country to another within a few hours, thanks to their thought.
Thomas A. Edison invented the light bulb. He got fed up with using candles and matches, and so he

thought of having something that would light up a room without using a candle and matches.

It is the same for Steve Jobs, the creator of Apple technology, and many others.

It all started with a *thought* that created all those things that we enjoy today.

Every single person is a creative centre and can create a thought. A thought that is held in mind will create a form.

Now, you might say," how can I think of an abundance when I am in debt"?

I know it is hard to do so, but you must do it. You must think thoughts of abundance to attract the abundance to you. Set up an automatic debt repayment scheme and don't think of debt anymore. You **must** switch yourself from thinking about debt to thinking about abundance.

You must understand that **your** thoughts brought that debt to you and, if you keep thinking about debt, you will only attract more debt. And that is not what you want. That is why you must think thoughts of abundance to attract more abundance. Don't worry yourself about HOW the debt will go away; leave the Universe to figure out the **how.** Your job is to think thoughts of abundance, thoughts of the rich life that you really want to live. Don't limit yourself by saying, 'I only want to get by; I don't need to be a millionaire.' That is the worst thing you can do. You must think like a millionaire to attract wealth to you. It is your right to be rich. There are no limits at all. The only limits are the ones that we impose on ourselves. Remember that!

And it is the same for every area of your life that you would like to improve.

If you want to make your current relationship better, think better thoughts of that relationship or, if you want to attract a man or woman into your life, think thoughts of that relationship as if you have it already.
I know it is hard to think about a nice relationship if you don't have one or to think about wealth when you have no money or very little money. It requires power to do it, but I want you to realize that you have enormous power within you. You are more powerful than you think! That is the truth, whether you believe It or not.
Also, don't listen to people who are complaining about their financial situation as you will give your attention to it, and that is what you will attract. Whenever you meet someone or hear somebody complaining about money or anything else, just walk away. Excuse yourself kindly and leave as fast as you can. Let me give you an example.
Do you remember a time when you thought about something that was bad, and the more you thought about it, the more of the same thoughts you attracted? The situation that looked bad, to begin with, started to look like the end of the world. Do you remember that? And that is what I am talking about here. Your thoughts are extremely powerful and, therefore, you must become aware of your thoughts and start using them to your advantage to create a life you truly desire. The life that you have been dreaming about but didn't know how to get. Now you do!
You are becoming aware of the power your thoughts have and know how to start thinking to create a wonderful life, just like I did and millions of

people around the world. Always remember that Your Pictures Create Your Life, and everything starts with a thought! Whatever pictures you hold in your mind, that's what you will get.
In the next chapter, I will explain what the 'mind' is and how it works.

"There is a thinking stuff from which all things are made, and which, in its original state, permeates, penetrates, and fills the interspaces of the universe. A thought in this substance produces the thing that is imaged by the thought.
You can form things in your thought, and by impressing your thought
upon formless substance, can cause the thing you think about to be created."
(Wallace D. Wattles)

CHAPTER 2

Mind

*"Your strongest muscle and worst enemy is your mind.
Train it well."*
(Anonymous)

Many people confuse themselves by thinking that "mind" is a brain. That is not the case. Mind is an activity; it is the unseen part of your personality. We have two parts of the mind. One part is 'conscious mind,' and the other is our 'sub-conscious mind.' We have mental faculties that are resident in our conscious mind. As I mentioned in Chapter 1, we have senses; we can hear, see, smell, taste, and touch.
Then, we have our intellectual faculties like imagination, intuition, memory, will, reason, and perception.
The majority of people use only their senses and not their higher faculties. They are not aware of them, and these are the factors that separate us from the animal kingdom.
Animals can see, hear, smell, taste, and touch, but they don't have the higher faculties. Only humans have them and, yet, so many don't use them.
It can be a bit confusing as no one has ever seen the mind, which is why, back in 1930's, Dr. Thurman Fleet decided to draw a picture of the mind to make it a bit easier for people to understand their mind by seeing a picture of it. It's

called a *stick person.*
Dr. Fleet drew a big circle and put a line across it in the middle and a line to go underneath (*see picture below*).
With the drawing of the stick person, people were able to get a better understanding and control of their mind.
Our conscious mind is our 'thinking mind.' That's where our ideas and dreams are formed.
The conscious mind can accept or reject information it receives. We get a lot of information from the news, radio, newspapers, or even from people that we associate with. It also stores the information that we have been 'given' when we were babies. I believe that most of this information was not at all good for us, but, as a baby, you have no ability to reject information. A baby is programmed to accept all these ideas as a fact.
Let's say that your parents used to tell you when you were a child that *"if you want to have money, you have to go to school and then you must get a good job, you must work hard to have money."*
That is not true at all, but, as you were being fed with those kinds of ideas, you grew up believing that if you wanted to have money, you had to work hard and have a good job.
Your parents didn't mean to give you bad ideas or give you false ideas. They just gave you what they had, what they thought was right or true. They probably inherited those ideas from their parents and their parents from theirs and so on… so, you can't really blame them for that. They were just giving you what they thought was the best.

But now, you are becoming aware of your mind and how to use your mind the right way. All those false ideas have formed your paradigm, and that paradigm created your life. But you can change it, and you can change it right now.

You are probably wondering, "what is Paradigm"? Paradigm is a multitude of **habits**, including other people's habits passed on from one generation to the next. This Paradigm controls our behaviour and our results. Fortunately, you can change it and, if you really want to change your life, you must change your paradigm.

So how do you change it? Through the repetition of information.

You should have an affirmation to help you with your paradigm. So, what is an affirmation? An affirmation is a statement which should always start with *I am so happy and grateful now that…* and then fill in the space with whatever it is that you want to change. Permit me to give you an example. Let's say that you don't have enough money, and your paradigm is telling you that "you can't have the money"; "who do you think you are,"? "You are not a millionaire and never will be." This is when an affirmation comes to the rescue.

You write down: *I am so happy and grateful now that money comes to me in increasing quantities on a continuous basis.*

Affirmations are very powerful, but you must repeat them at least 1000 times a day, every day. Keep repeating the affirmation over and over and over. At first, your mind will be a bit reluctant to accept it (and that is absolutely normal), but as long as you keep repeating it every single day, you will start to believe it, and that is when you will start to form a new habit - a new paradigm. Please don't give up on it because you don't see a change right away! You must hold on to your faith. You must believe that what you are reading is true. Let me tell you that if you kept telling yourself a lie over and over, you would start believing in that lie!

I tried it when I started my journey with affirmations, and it became my life. I read my affirmation over and over and over every single day, and one day I really felt that it was true.

You can have several affirmations for other areas of your life and keep repeating them all every single day, 1000 times a day. I guarantee you; you will change your paradigm. Is it easy? No, it's not. If it were, everyone would be doing it but, if you really want to see a change and get new results, you have to do it. And, of course, you must discipline yourself. Discipline is the ability to give yourself a command and then follow it.

Discipline is vitally important when changing your paradigm. Say to yourself, " I am going to do this, no matter what." Once you have decided to change your life, you are halfway there.

The second part of our mind is the 'sub-conscious' mind, which is also referred to as an 'emotional mind.' This part of you is the most magnificent. It is the power centre and functions within every cell of your body.

Every thought that your conscious mind chooses to accept will also be accepted by the sub-conscious mind. Your sub-conscious mind has no ability to reject. That is why we should be very careful of what we are planting in our mind.

The great thing about our sub-conscious mind is that it cannot differentiate whether something is real or imagined. In other words, whatever you plant in your mind, whether it is real/true or not, that is what you will get.

Let's say that you are letting the outside world control you, e.g., you are talking to your friend about not having enough money, and you are getting emotional about it, that is precisely what you will get. You will always be short of money because that is what you are planting in your mind. You are getting emotionally involved with it, so you will get it.

However, if you are talking about something that you don't have yet, for example, you want to have £10,000 in your account, and you are talking about money with confidence and feel good about it, as if you had the money already, you will get it - because that is the picture you are creating in your marvellous mind and you are getting emotionally involved with the idea of having money. And that is the picture that will materialize in your life!

We are the creators of our lives, and we can create whatever we want if we don't let the outside world control us. Our mind has enormous power, and whatever we plant, we will get. Whether people believe in it or understand it or not.

It is also important to be mindful of our self-talk. Your mind is listening and giving you exactly what you plant in it, whether it is good or bad.

Then, we also have a third part called Body. This is the most obvious part of you; however, it is only the house you live in.

Every single thought or picture that you plant in your mind will express itself through your body into action, and these actions will determine your results.

First, you create a picture in your conscious mind, and then you get emotionally involved with it (feelings). Those feelings will move you into action, and the action will give you the results. If those results are not what you want, then you must change them, and to change your results, you must change your pictures, feelings, and actions.

Once you grasp the understanding of your mind, it will become simple, and you will be able to create the life that you truly want to live—a life with no limitations or negative emotions. Make sure you are creating wonderful pictures and start today!

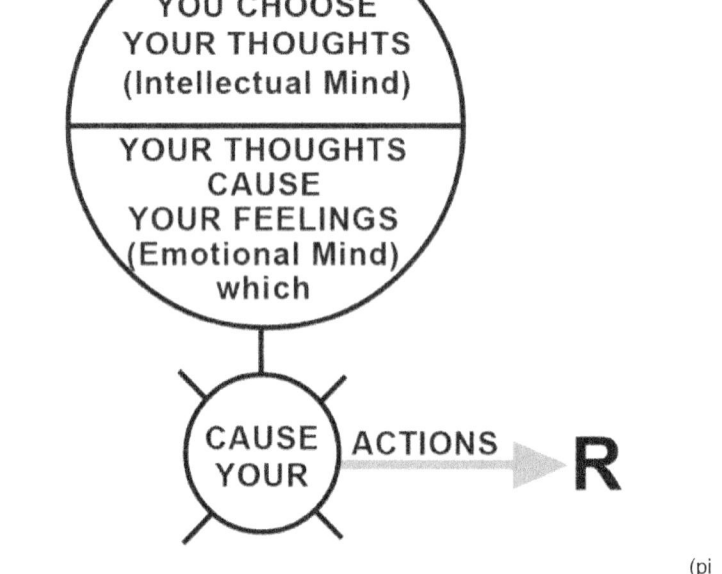

(picture from PGI)

CHAPTER 3

Faith

" Faith is a state of mind which may be induced or created
by affirmation or repeated instructions to the sub-conscious mind,
through the principle of autosuggestion".
(Napoleon Hill)

Faith is a very powerful positive emotion. In fact, faith, love, and sex are the most powerful of all the positive emotions.
Faith is something that you must develop if you want to change your life in order to achieve absolutely anything in your life. You must have faith to believe that you can get whatever you want.
To develop faith, you must train it. The best way to do it is by autosuggestion. You can use affirmations - any affirmations that you like. Let me give you an example here.
Let's say that you want to have a continuous flow of money. You can make an affirmation like this: "I am so happy and grateful now that money comes to me in huge quantities from multiple sources on a continuous basis" or "I am a money magnet or money comes to me easily and frequently."
This is an affirmation that I like to use to attract money, and it works.
You must keep repeating it every single day, 1000 times a day, or more. The more you repeat it, the

more you start developing your faith. You will start to believe that the statement is true, and once that real belief is there, you will see your financial situation changing.

You may remember your mother or grandmother saying, "*If you see a black cat, it is bad luck.*" And is it really bad luck? No, it is not. It is just something that we believe in because we have been programmed to believe that it is true. There are many other beliefs out there that people have without any real proof. If you can believe in something like that, you can train yourself to believe in anything you want. If you want more money, train yourself with affirmations to believe in what you are reading. It works for everything that you might want, not just money.

I remember when I was starting with this way of thinking.

I wanted to be a criminal Barrister. I was not a confident person at all, and I didn't really believe that I could become a successful barrister in the UK, especially as I was from a different country. But it was my dream, and Bob said to me, "*You can be or do or have anything that you want, you just must believe that you can. Start to believe, and you are halfway there*".

I will never forget these words, and that was precisely what I did.

I wrote the affirmation, "*I am so happy and grateful now that I am a successful criminal barrister in England and Wales,*" and I kept reading it over and over, every single day. All-day long, I would have this affirmation in my head, and I started to believe that I was a successful Barrister. I could see myself in a courtroom wearing a Barrister's gown and wig and defending my clients. It felt so real.

And now I am training to become a Barrister. Not only that, but I am also working alongside one of the top criminal Barristers in England. I have no doubt whatsoever that I will become a phenomenal barrister.

Thanks to my newly formed belief, I was able to attract this fantastic Barrister, Anthony, into my life. I learn from Anthony, and I am so grateful to have him in my life. He is such a blessing.

Your faith is vitally important. Whether you are working towards something or whether it is your self-image (the way you see yourself) that you want to improve, faith is the **key.** Faith gives power and action to your thought.

Have faith in yourself. Become aware of your true power within, believe, and know that you can have anything that you desire.

You must believe. You must have faith.

Faith is the starting point of all riches; it is the start of all miracles.

We all know that when we read a statement which is either true or a lie, if we read it often enough, we will start to believe in it, and it will become the truth. You know, that faith based on understanding will move mountains. It is the ability to see the invisible; to believe in the incredible, and it will let us to see what others call impossible.

Once you have developed faith in yourself and in your power within you, you will be unstoppable. You will see all those great things coming to you because you have faith.

" Faith is taking the first step, even when you don't see the whole staircase."
(Martin Luther King Jr.)

CHAPTER 4

Gratitude

*" Gratitude is an attitude that hooks us up to our source of supply. And
the more grateful you are, the closer you become to your maker, to
the architect of the Universe, to the spiritual core of your being.
It's a phenomenal lesson".*
(Bob Proctor)

Gratitude is the process of mental adjustment and atonement.
We know that we should be grateful for what we have or for the help that we receive. But are we really grateful? You might say, "Yes, I am grateful. I do say thank you".
Well, you might say thank you to people, BUT do you really feel that profound gratitude inside?
We are programmed to say thank you, please, etc. It is what we have been taught to say to be polite towards other people, but real gratitude is something that you feel inside. It is a great feeling, a genuine feeling of being truly thankful for something or to someone.
You could be grateful for a nice cup of coffee. You could feel so happy, so great that you can have that cup of coffee. There are so many things that we

take for granted instead of being grateful for them. Now, with COVID 19, we have become so grateful for a hairdresser, for our freedom (to be able to go out), and for so many other things.

Did you ever realise how important a hairdresser is? Having to experience lockdown makes you realise how grateful you are to be able to have your hair done. Right?

I believe this lockdown has done us good in a way. It made us appreciate things so much more. People started to be more aware of things that they used to take for granted and became more kind. And yes, there are still many people who were complaining all the way through the lockdown, and instead of doing something that they enjoy doing, they became even more unhappy. That is really sad because if situations like this don't make people appreciate what they have, I don't think that those people will ever WAKE UP!

A person that is grateful is the winner!

A grateful person is working with the Universal Law and will be rewarded in accordance to their grateful heart. A person that is not grateful will never experience those feelings of joy, happiness, love. That is why we all must be grateful and not only when it suits us!

We must be grateful and feel the gratitude all the time. The grateful mind is always fixed upon the best and will always receive the best.

Many people have ordered their lives the right way, and yet they are still suffering with poverty. Do you

want to know why? Because of their lack of gratitude.
It is very simple, but not many people realise it. Very often, people make a huge mistake. As soon as they receive one gift from God (or whoever or whatever they believe in), they will cut the cord with Him and don't give any acknowledgement. Then they wonder, Why me? Why me again? It's because gratitude is what brings the riches to You. Never make the same mistake! The more you are grateful for what you have, the more you will receive.
Let's say you have a car which is fairly old, and you would like a new car. First, you must be grateful for your old car to be able to receive the new one. If you are not grateful for the car you have, you will not receive the one you want. It's that simple.
And it is the same with your job. I know many people that complain about their jobs and moan that they cannot find a new one. It is obvious that until they are grateful for their current job, they will not find a new one. No matter how good they are or how hard they are trying, they will stay exactly where they are because of their lack of gratitude. I know this from my own experience. I had a job that I did not like, but I knew that to get the job I wanted, I first had to become grateful for my current job. So, I started to give thanks every day for my job. I even started to look for things in the job that I did enjoy, and I gave thanks for them too. I really felt the gratitude inside of me. It shifted my mood to a

better frequency, and I felt much calmer.
Not long after, I got the exact job that I wanted! Can you see how easy it can be to get what you want if you are grateful? We cannot just use plain words like 'thank you' without a true feeling of gratitude.
We must develop the feeling of being grateful and then watch the magic happen. The mental attitude of gratitude brings us closer to the infinite power from which the blessings come. Gratitude can shift you from a negative state of mind into a positive state. Sometimes, when I don't feel the way I want to feel when I feel a negative vibe coming to me, and I know I must be in a positive state of mind to feel happy, I always start to write down the things that I am grateful for. This simple exercise always helps me to move into that positive state of mind, and, as you become positive, you will start to attract positive people, events into your life. And I am sure that that is what you want. Nobody wants to attract negative people or events into their lives. And this simple exercise will help you.
I included gratitude in my morning routine. Every morning when I wake up, I write down 10 things that I am grateful for. And I don't just write them down, but I also ask myself, 'why am I grateful for this'? That makes me think, and it makes my gratitude even deeper!
The best thing is that you can write down the things that you have that you are grateful for, and you can also write the things that you do not have yet.

Gratitude will help you to get those things even quicker! Isn't that great? I absolutely love it. Include the gratitude exercise in YOUR morning routine and during the day if you find yourself shifting into a negative frequency. Change it straightaway. Use gratitude! Any time and as many times as you like.

We must realise that to get what we want; we must first become grateful. I will get back to this morning routine again in Chapter 7.

" Gratitude is the single most important ingredient to living a successful and fulfilled life."
(Jack Canfield)

CHAPTER 5

Goals

" Set your goals high and don't stop till you get there."
(Bo Jackson)

What are goals? Something on a football match that you attended, right?
Yes, but the goals I am going to talk about in this chapter are very different. These goals can change your life completely when you set them correctly and then go after them using the way that I am going to recommend.
Goals are our desires, something that we want to get. You can have everything you want when you understand how to become a goal achiever.
What is a goal achiever? A goal achiever is a person who sets a goal and goes after it, not stopping until they get it! You can become a goal achiever when you follow the process I am about to explain.
To become a Goal Achiever, you must decide what you want and make a decision to get what you want (without breaching the rights of others).
Think of the lifestyle you would have if you could get any goal that you desire. Where would you live? What car would you drive? What clothes would you wear? Where would you go on holiday? Where would you work, or what business would you have? I want you to really think about these questions and

take them seriously. Read each question several times and answer it either in your head or on a piece of paper. And DO NOT limit yourself! Go wild with your desires because you can have them when you really want them, and it doesn't matter what they are!

There is no size for the Universe; nothing is cheap nor expensive; nothing is big or small; the only limits that exist are the ones that we set. So, don't set any! Go absolutely wild as you answer those questions.

To set a goal, you must really think about something that you truly want. It must be something special. It has to be important to you, and you don't have to justify to anyone why you want it.

When you choose the proper goal, everything will start to change in your life. You will start to develop your conscious awareness as you move closer to your goal, which is great as we need to become consciously aware so that we can change our 'old bad habits' and replace them with the positive new ones.

To be able to do this, you must have a good reason, and the reason is Your Goal.

I remember when I set a goal for the first time in my life. I was 33 years old. Up until then, I was just cruising, like a ship without a radar. I was just following the majority and achieved almost nothing. But then, when I set my goal, everything started to change.

Bob told me to set a goal that I really wanted to achieve. So, I did. I wrote down my goal, which was my dream house.

Now, at that time, my yearly income was around £15,000, and my dream house was for sale for £875,000. I had no idea how I was going to get that house, but, as a good student of Bob Proctor, I did exactly what he told me.

I didn't really believe that I could get that house, but I could see that Bob, Pixie, and Kathy did. To cut a long story short, I have that house! I kept my faith that my goal would come true, and it did. If I can do it - so can you!

Now, let me give you a few steps to follow to set a right goal.

There are 3 types of goals. 'A-type,' 'B-type,' and 'C-type.'

An 'A-type' goal is something that you know how to get. This would not be a good goal as there would be no personal growth at all, and we know that we set goals to grow. We want to see personal growth that we can only achieve by setting the right goals.

Next, we have 'B-type' goals. This is a goal that we **might** know how to get. This wouldn't be a good goal either as there would be no or only minimal growth.

Then, we have 'C-type' goals, which are the ones that we have absolutely no idea how to achieve. This is the type of goal you want to go after. With the 'C-type' goal, there is enormous growth along the way. That is what we want, and our goal becomes the reward for the growth we have accomplished.

So, set a C-type goal!

But how do you know what goal is the right one (because you want too many things at once)? Don't worry; I was the same.

First: Write down on a piece of paper ten things that you really want. Don't forget we are setting a C-type goal so go wild with your desires. You can call it 'MY SHOPPING LIST.'

Second: Now, prioritize your ten desires in order of importance where number 1 is the most important and number 10 the least important.

Third: Your number 1 goal is going to be your most important goal, and you are going to give it all your conscious attention! This is the goal you are going to write on your goal card.

Finally: Once you have written your goal on a goal card, carry it everywhere with you. Read it every single day, at least a thousand times a day, and truly feel as if you have already reached your goal. I have several goal cards with the same goal written on them, and I always carry one with me. I often change my bag or my trousers, so I have put a goal card in every pocket, so my goal is always with me. I read it every single morning for five minutes, and I really feel the feelings of having reached my goal. I do the same at night just before I go to bed.
Also, every time I put my hand in my pocket, there is my goal card, and so I read it again. Having my goal card in my pocket triggers a good feeling in my body, and so every time I touch it, I also feel great. I suggest you do the same. It is vitally important to get in alignment with your goal so it can manifest. Also, don't forget, your goal must be specific. You cannot just say, "I want a house in Florida." It is not

specific, and you could be very disappointed with the result. You must be specific, and choose the exact house that you want or at least the exact location where you want your house to be. It is the same principle for the car you want or the business you want to have.

You must be specific and give exact details of what you really want. I was very specific with my house. I knew I wanted that house, and so I wrote on my goal card the full address of the house I wanted. Always remember to start your sentence by saying, "I am so happy and grateful now that...." (*fill in the blank with your goal*) and, on the top of your goal card, write a date by which you want your goal to manifest, but keep in mind that you are just guessing the date. It might come right on the date or earlier or even after the date that you wrote down. However, do not get discouraged if your goal doesn't come to you by the date you wrote down and DO NOT change your goal. Change the date, extend the date for another year, and as long as you keep your faith and gratitude, you will get your goal. Allow yourself to relax, let yourself feel yourself in possession of your goal and talk, walk, and act as if you already have your goal.

Now, you might be asking, "what about the rest of my goals on my shopping list"? Do not worry about them. They will come along as you are working on your main goal.

Are you wondering, "How"? It is not for you to worry about the "how." Let the Universe/ God/ Buddha or whoever you believe in to worry about that. Your job is to set a goal, believe you can have it, and walk, talk, and act as if you already have it.

Vitally important is to know how to visualise your desire and to see yourself with your desire. I will explain how to use visualisation in the next chapter.

"The worst bankrupt in the world is the person who has lost his enthusiasm."
(H.W. Arnold)

CHAPTER 6

Visualisation

"When you visualize, then you materialize."
(Denis Waitley)

You are probably curious to know what visualisation is and why it is so important.
Visualisation has been referred to as dreaming for a long time (and still is). It could be called dreaming as you are visualising your desire, but it is not like dreaming that you are familiar with. Visualisation is a different form of dreaming.
I mentioned in the previous chapter that when you set a goal, you must then visualise. You must see yourself with that goal. What does that mean? It means that you have to close your eyes and visualise (see yourself) with your desire already in your possession. This visualisation exercise keeps your mind in order and brings your desired goal to you!
If you keep deliberately practising this exercise and properly examining your picture, you will get the picture in an exact form. Once you understand this power to visualise, it will bring you what you want. You will attract everything that you need in order to bring your picture into your material world.
Don't forget that everything is first formed in our mind. The pictures that we hold in our minds are the ones that will form our world. Whether the pictures are good or bad, they will manifest.
Visualising is the great secret to success. Every

single human being visualizes whether they know it or believe it or not. All the great inventions that we enjoy today have been nothing but a thought, a desire, a goal of someone. I mentioned The Wright Brothers and other inventors in Chapter 1, and I will repeat them again so you can really understand what I am trying to say to you.

The Wright Brothers are the ones who created a plane! They didn't have any special education. They were just two bicycle mechanics, BUT they had a dream. They had a desire to have this thing that would take them up in the sky. Everyone thought they had lost their mind for suggesting that they could fly. And had they lost their mind? No! Today, we can fly thanks to their phenomenal idea. They didn't know how they were going to do it, but they knew that if they could see themselves with that machine flying high, it would manifest. Everyone around them told them that it couldn't be done! Did they listen to those people? No, they did not. They were working with their higher faculties. They understood the visualisation.

Who do you think was the first person ever to conceive of a bicycle? It was Leonardo Da Vinci! Not only that, but he also had outstanding, notable achievements during his life, including a parachute that he designed in 1485. Alexander Graham Bell invented the telephone. Henry Ford invented the first V-8 motor. Henry's employees said it was impossible to invent it, but he told them to go and do it. After six months, they came back again and said it couldn't be done, but he did not listen to them. He formed a picture of the motor in his mind, and he knew that if he kept the picture in his mind,

it could be done. And it was!
What a phenomenal people. I introduced these great men to you because they are my absolute favourites, but there are many more.
Now, can you see what I am trying to say to you? Why am I telling you about these fantastic people? It is for You to realise that, whatever it is that you want, you can have it. It doesn't matter how impossible it seems to you or to someone else. Also, bear in mind that you DO NOT listen to anybody who tells you it can't be done. Those people are operating with a limited mind, which is fine for them, but it is not your limit.
Remember, there are no limits whatsoever unless we impose them upon ourselves. Every time I write a goal, I am very specific about it. As well as writing down my goal, I also describe it precisely, so the Universe knows what exactly I want.
I have a notepad in which I describe every single goal that I want to achieve, and I read it daily. The reason is so it will get properly fixed in my mind, and then I do my visualising.
I see myself already having my goal. As I mentioned, my very first goal was to own the house that I wanted so much. I went to view the house, so I knew what it looked like from the inside. Curtis thought I was crazy, but that did not stop me. As I was walking from one room to another, I was visualising myself already living in the house. Then, I came home, and I wrote down very precisely how I wanted every room to look. What floor would I have; what door; what room colour; what bed. I even changed the kitchen in my mind and added a

pool and gym in the garden! My description was five pages long.

Can you see how important it is to get precise with your picture? You must visualise every day. Every morning, night, and also during the day. Always have your picture, your desire, in your mind, and when visualising, see yourself having that desire already in your possession. Feel exactly how you would feel if you had your goal. Your feelings, your full faith (faith with gratitude), and visualisation are vitally important when creating your world.

Is it going to be easy? No. That's why you have to keep practising this visualisation exercise so you can become a master at it, and you will!

Never doubt yourself. Doubt is a negative feeling, and you must stay positive in order to manifest your desires. Have faith and know that you will get what you asked for. It always works with every person, every time. Practise the visualisation, and you will create a wonderful life.

" If you can see it in your mind, you will hold it in your hand."
(Bob Proctor)

CREATIVE BEINGS
VOCALIZING
AFFIRMATIONS
PRESENT TENSE
WRITTEN DOWN
REPEATED STATEMENT
POSITIVE THINKING
HEAL
CHANGING THOUGHTS
RE-PROGRAM
VISUALISATION
PERSONAL
GOALS
WE CREATE OUR WORLD
HEALING BELIEFS
SPECIFIC
SELF-EMPOWERMENT
HAPPINESS
POSITIVE
PEACE
SUCCESS
CHANGING BELIEFS
NEW THOUGHTS

CHAPTER 7

Routine & Discipline

*" You will never change your life until you change something you do
daily.
The secret of your success is found in your daily routine".*
(John C. Maxwell)

I have mentioned Routine and Discipline in previous chapters, and now I will explain them in more detail, so you know what they exactly mean and the benefits of including them in your life. It is very simple, but it is not easy. However, you can do it!
Every successful person, whether past or present, had a routine. You are probably asking, "what routine did they have, and why did they have it"? Routine is something that you do daily. You have to start your day right for it to become a successful and great day. I did not have any specific routine, just the usual ones that I am sure we all have, such as going food shopping every Friday, etc. However, since I started to study with Bob Proctor, I have developed a routine that keeps me motivated and excited every single day.
It took me a long time to get used to it. At first, my old paradigm (old habits-bad habits) kept kicking in and telling me, "stay in bed you are tired,"; "have a rest,"; "don't read, watch Netflix instead." Oh dear, it

was hard, but I overpowered my old paradigm with my new positive paradigm. Now, I have formed my daily routine. I wake up every morning at 4:30 am (no exceptions!), and the first thing I do is meditation. Your mind is still sleepy when you get up and starting to wake up slowly, so it's a great time to meditate and put your mind into a good, positive vibration. I use my favourite Buddhist meditation, but you can use any meditation music you like, and there is plenty to choose from on YouTube.

I usually meditate for 30 minutes in the morning, and then I do my visualisation. I visualise the life I want to live, exactly how I want it to be. And I visualise every area of my life.

Remember Chapter 6. Go back to it and read it over and over until you see the magic of visualisation. Once I have finished my visualisation, I practice gratitude. As I mentioned in the gratitude chapter, I write down ten things that I am grateful for, and for each one that I write, I always ask myself, "why am I grateful for this"? Then I start to think of the answer.

The reason for doing this is, as you think about why you are grateful, you are getting deeper feelings of gratitude, and your gratitude is becoming more powerful.

I don't just list the things that I already have; I also list the things that I don't have yet. This is so powerful because you are giving thanks in advance for something that you want. You feel as if you have it already, and it brings it to you even faster! Isn't it fantastic?

Then, I read out my affirmations. I read my main

affirmation (my goal) for five minutes and the rest of my affirmations for three minutes. Then I send love to three people that bother me. I say their name and say, "… I am sending you my love". I really try to feel as much love as possible. This is a very good exercise if you have someone who bothers you. As soon as you send them love (which I know can be very hard with some people), you feel much calmer and have a better feeling inside. And always remember that you are not doing it for them, but for yourself.
Instead of cursing them and keeping hate in my body, I always forgive everyone who bothers me. If you are cursing the other person, you are harming yourself. It's like drinking poison and expecting the other person to die. It will never happen!
Make sure you do this forgiveness/sending love exercise.
After that, I do yoga. I love yoga. Once I have finished yoga, I read my self-image (the way I want to see myself), and then I read a book for 10-15 minutes. I end my morning routine by reading the six things that I want to do that day. I always write them down before I go to bed, so they are there for me to see in the morning. They are six things that I must do during a day so that I can get closer to my goal. One of those things was to write my book – the book you are reading now.
I always make sure I do them all and, if for some reason I didn't do one of them, I would do them the next day. And after I finished my morning routine and reviewed my 6 action steps, I start my day. And then at night, I read a book again and give thanks for all the good things that happened during the

day. Then I meditate for an hour or so and then go to sleep.

Was it easy to develop this morning routine? No, it was very hard, and that's when discipline is needed. You must discipline yourself in order to develop your routine and stay on track.

Previously, I mentioned that discipline is the ability to give yourself a command and follow it. No matter what. No excuses.

Your old paradigm will put up a great fight, but remember that you are forming a new paradigm which is stronger than your old one. If you want to win, you can win.

Whenever you find yourself slipping back to the 'old you' version, look at your goal card. That is your PUSH to remind you why you are doing everything that you are doing. It is going to be hard, but it is doable.

I have done it. Bob has done it. Sandy has done it. Albert Einstein has done it, and millions around the world have done it. And you can do it too. You must discipline yourself to be able to move from where you are now to where you want to be. Say to yourself, "I am doing this" and "I can, and I will do it"! Keep saying that to yourself over and over. If you really want your goal, you will discipline yourself. You will not try to find any excuses. Discipline is something you can develop with practise and, the more you practise, the better you will become at it.

Here are three things that Bob suggested to get started.

- ✓ Realize that if you want something different in your life, you must do things differently. Then command yourself to do what must be done.
- ✓ Start to schedule your day from the time you wake up until you go to bed.
- ✓ Hold the image of being successful at what you want to do.

As I said, it won't be easy, but you will get stronger and stronger day by day. You will notice that you are able to do more when you control your days. And don't just think of what you can do today. Do it! Write down your daily routine right now. Not tomorrow, not next week, but NOW. Give yourself a command that you are going to do it and do it.

Also, the time you wake up at is vitally important. Every great achiever wakes up early in the morning. They don't stay in bed till 8 am, or 10 am! They get up early so they can use their time productively.

In the next chapter, I will explain what self-image is and how to use it.

"Discipline is the No.1 delineating factor between the rich, the middle class, and the poor".
(Robert Kiyosaki)

CHAPTER 8

Self-image

" There is only one corner of the Universe you can be certain of improving, and this is your own self".
(Aldous Huxley)

I am sure you are wondering now, "what is self-image"? You may not have heard of it yet, and that's fine; I will now explain what it is and how it affects your life.

Self-image is the image you hold of yourself. I don't mean the image that you see when you look in a mirror. The image you see in the mirror is the reflection of your physical being. That's not how you see You.

You see You in your mind based on information that you have about You. Some people have a lot of false information about themselves, so they have a very false self-image.

Your self-image is what you think of You.

If you think you are not nice, or you are fat, or you are not worthy, and so on, you have a false self-image, which is not a good self-image at all. It will control your behaviour, your actions, and everything that you do.

If you are a salesperson, your sales are not going to go up; instead, they will go down because of the image you hold of yourself.

But if a person has a good self-image, they see

themselves being nice, attractive, productive, and so on. They will become a magnet for great things to come to them because they hold a good self-image.

Can you see why self-image is so important? My self-image was very poor for nearly 30 years. It only changed when I met Bob.

During our Q&A's, Bob got me to look at the results I was getting in my life, and he asked me how I saw myself.

At first, I didn't understand what he meant by that, and I was too proud to ask, "what do you mean Bob"?

Back then, my results weren't changing, and I wanted to know why. This question came back to my mind when I spoke to Andres, and so I asked him, and he explained what Bob meant.

It was that 'ah-ha' moment. It all made sense, and I could see why I wasn't changing. My self-image was stopping me.

Self-image is based in our sub-conscious mind. It's a part of our paradigm, and we know that paradigm is a multitude of habits (mostly bad habits in my case back then).

I knew that to get different results in my life; I had to alter my self-image.

I am sure your self-image is what is stopping you from getting, doing, and being whatever you want. Am I right? I want you to really think about this question.

Don't just read this chapter. Really think about what you are reading and ask yourself, "what is the image I hold of myself"?

Ask yourself this question and seriously think about

the answer. As I mentioned, my self-image was not good, so I sat down and wrote down everything that I wanted myself to be like. I wrote down all the greatest qualities that a person can have, and then I read it every single day. I would read my self-image out loud every morning and night.

After a while, I started to feel like that person in my self-image. I started to develop all the qualities that I had written down. That's what is going to happen to you when you write down your self-image and read it daily.

You will start to believe that what you read is true, and you will become that person. You must read it and believe that you already possess those qualities.

At the beginning, you might won't even know what to write down or what qualities you would like to have, but, as you really think about who you want to be and what kind of person you really want to be, you will know exactly what to write.

It is vitally important to form a new self-image when you are operating with a poor image.

Since I changed my self-image, my whole life started to change. I felt more confident, and I felt much better about myself, especially when I looked in the mirror. Instead of finding faults with myself, I was able to compliment the person I saw in the mirror. I still read my self-image every single day, and I alter it to include other qualities that I want to have. It works wonders.

Here are a few examples of how to start writing your self-image.

- I AM calm
- I AM happy
- I AM blessed
- I AM abundant
- I AM fearless
- I AM a millionaire
- I AM healthy
- I AM a good mother/father
- I AM a fantastic wife/husband
- I AM a success in everything I do
- My income is getting higher and higher
- People seek me out to do business with me
- My business is increasing daily
- I AM generous
- I AM …. (*fill in the blank*)

These are just some examples that you can use in your self-image. Write down everything that you want to be like and read it daily. You will become that person with those qualities, and your life will change dramatically!

To change your world, you must first change the way you see you, your self-image.

"It's not who you are that holds you back, it's who you think you are not".
(Sandy Gallagher)

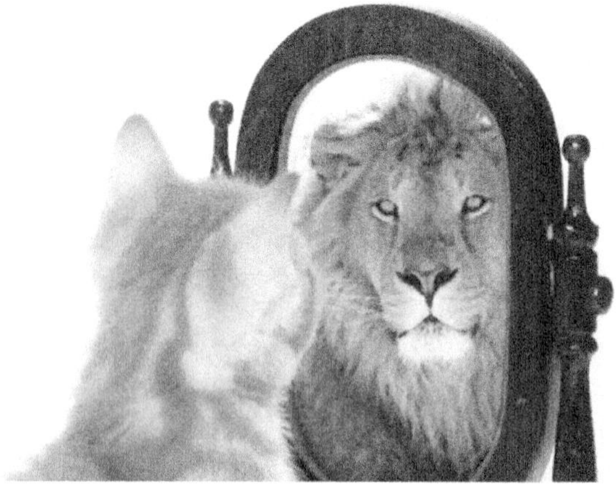

CHAPTER 9

Thinking and Acting in "The Certain Way"

*"Men acquire a particular quality by constantly acting
in a particular way".*
(Aristotle)

What is thinking and acting in the 'Certain Way'? Well, this is the real magic.
It means that you must **think** and **act** in a way that you want to live. Let me explain this in more detail. Thinking in 'the certain way' is to form a clear picture of your desire. You must think of what it is that you truly want. It is not enough to just say, "I want to have plenty of money," or "I want to travel," or "I want to have a good job" or "I want a new car." If you want to impress your desires upon your thinking, you must be very specific, very detailed. When you say "plenty," your thinking substance doesn't know what 'plenty' is for you. What is 'plenty' for you can be very little for others, and what can happen is that you can get £100, which is 'plenty' for one and very little for others. So, you must be very specific about what it is that you want. If it is money that you want, write down the exact amount that you wish to have in your account. Keep that thought, that desire, with you at all times. Spend as much time as you can, forming that picture, seeing it in your mind as a sure thing.

The clearer and more detailed you make your picture, the stronger it gets. The stronger it gets, the easier it will be to hold it in your mind.
Don't forget that you are not only a dreamer. You must have a purpose to realize it. You must live mentally in a way as if you have your desire already. Once you have formed a clear picture, I guarantee you; you will see it materialize.
 I love this quote from the Bible: '*Whatsoever things you ask for when you pray, believe that you receive them, and you shall have them.*'
This is precisely the right quote for this chapter. Get that picture of your desire into your mind and imagine having it already. Make use of your imagination.
I remember when my son wanted PS4 for Christmas, I said to him, "form a picture of it in your mind and play with it as if you have it."
At first, he was not happy, as he wanted to hold it in his hands (which is what every eight-year-old wants), but my point was for him to realize that he could have it as long as he worked in accordance with Universal Laws.
For him, it was not that hard to do, as he saw me doing it with my desires. So, he did it. He really used his imagination to help him with it.
He drew a picture of the PS4 and put it in the place that he wanted his PS4 to be. He even mentally played with it, and he had lots of different games too.
Then, when Christmas came along, he gave me a list for Father Christmas, and PS4 was not on it! When I asked him why he hadn't written PS4 on his list, he said, "I only need a new game for it, mum. I

can't imagine how to play it as I have only heard about it at school".

Can you see what my son was doing? He was using his higher faculties, and so he didn't even notice that he had no PS4 because he was playing with it in his imagination. He had it in his mind!

He did exactly the same with WWE VIP tickets, and this is exactly how we all must use our minds, our higher faculties. We must start to think in 'the certain way' and remember to have faith and be grateful for it in advance.

Thinking in 'the certain way' will bring you riches, but you must also take personal action. You must act in 'the certain way' as well as think in 'the certain way.'

To act in 'the certain way' is to act now! Not in the past or the future but NOW. Act as if you have your desire already in your possession.

Let's say you want to have a job as a teacher. You should see yourself doing that job already. If you are an apprentice or teaching assistant, you can do it while you are at work. See yourself as a teacher. Hear parents and colleagues call you, Teacher. See your name written down, and underneath see your job title – Teacher.

If you don't have a job and want to be a teacher, go and study to become one. Nowadays, you can do online courses and still do everything else that you want to. I have done it, and so can you.

Write yourself a job offer from the school where you want to work and give yourself a great offer. Write down the position that you want and how much you want to earn. Write down what days and hours you want to work. Be very specific. See yourself

accepting the offer and shaking hands with your new boss.
Make it so vivid in your mind that it will have to materialize.
If it is a business that you want to have or if you want to improve your current one, see it as already being the way you want it to be, regardless of appearances.
We know that to bring riches into our lives, we must work from the inside out and not from the outside in. Everything starts from the inside, and so, whatever you desire, you must see it in your mind clearly and act as if you have it already.
Reread my son's short story. It will help you and show you what to do if you are still not sure.
In summary, get a clear and detailed picture of your desire. **Think** and **act** in 'the certain way,' which is *as if you have it NOW.*

"It is not your part to guide or supervise the creative process.
All you have to do with that is to retain your vision, stick to
your purpose and maintain your faith and gratitude".
(Wallace D. Wattles)

CHAPTER 10

How to Calm Your Mind

*"Calm mind brings inner strength and self-confidence, so that's
very important for good health".*
(Dalai Lama)

I am sure everyone wants to know how to calm their minds, especially at times of stress or worry, or perhaps you fear something.
As I have already explained, the **mind** is not your brain; it is an activity.
It always works. It never stops. Even when you go to sleep, your mind is still working, and that is why it is vitally important to know how to calm your mind.
When you are worried or fear something, the best thing you can do is face your fear; otherwise, you will never get rid of it.
Whatever it is that you are afraid of, face it. Worry is fear, and fear is a negative emotion!
If you are stressed or not having a good day, the best way to help yourself is to sit down in a comfortable chair or on the sofa, close your eyes and take a deep breath. I take three deep breaths, but you can take as many as you like. Then turn on some meditation music, keep your eyes closed and let yourself relax.
Relax, and don't think of anything. Just relax and concentrate on the music. This is the best way for your mind to relax.

I meditate every day, every morning at 4:30 am. I meditate for 30 minutes and then at night for 1 hour.
If you never tried meditation, you can start with 5-10 minutes a day. Those few minutes of meditation will change your mood rapidly. Then as you get into it, increase the timings. Go from 10 minutes to 15 minutes, and then from 15 minutes to 20 minutes and so on.
You can meditate as much as you like and for as long as you like. Meditation is a great tool to develop. Your mind will become much calmer and more creative and productive. When you meditate every morning, your days will be filled with a lot of energy, and you will feel amazing. Even if someone or something is not so great, you will not react to it. Instead, you will be responding, and your mind will be at peace, in nice, calm order.
If you suffer with depression or anxiety, then you should definitely meditate. Often when I see people who are depressed, I ask them why they are depressed. They say it's their money situation or their relationship, etc. Then I ask them if they meditate. I sometimes get a very funny look from them, but then I explain how powerful meditation is, and when they try it, they really see the difference.
I had a friend who was always stressed and chasing time. I told her to stop and meditate. She told me she didn't have time to meditate, so I said to her, "this is exactly why you must stop and meditate."
She was very reluctant to do it, but she tried it, and she loved it, and she has been meditating every single day since.

She says she feels great, and she doesn't feel like she must rush and that she even seems to have a spare time, so she joined a gym. Isn't it great!
I was so happy to hear that. It's brilliant.
I want the same for you. I want you to feel great, happy, amazing, doing whatever you want to do, and going wherever you want to go. Life is so incredible when we do everything that we want to do, but first, you must bring order to your mind. You must train your mind to stay calm, and meditation is the way to do that. Get into the habit of meditating. Meditate every day, and you will see the difference in you and in your actions.
Start meditating today. You will be so glad you did.

*"The goal of meditation is not to control your thoughts,
it's to stop
letting them control you".*
(The Age of Enlightenment)

Epilogue

The purpose of this short book is to help people live the life they truly desire. To make you realize that YOUR PICTURES CREATE YOUR LIFE.
Make sure you only hold good pictures in your mind and pay no attention to anything that does not serve you or grows you.
This book is written in simple language so that everyone can understand the context, even children.
Please share this book with your children, grandchildren, brothers, sisters, and friends. Share it with your neighbours and with everyone that you know.
And you can be sure that their life and your life will change.
Finally, don't just read this book. Study it. Really think about what you are reading, and you will change your life.
I have done it, and so can you.

To Your Success,

Klaudia S. W

BOOKS for FURTHER READING

- You Were Born Rich (by Bob Proctor)
- The Demand Principle (by Peggy McColl)
- Success Through A Positive Mental Attitude (by Napoleon Hill and Clement Stone)
- How to Stop Worrying and Start Living (by Dale Carnegie)
- The Science of Getting Rich (by Wallace D. Wattles)
- Think and Grow Rich (by Napoleon Hill)
- The Master Key System (by Charles F. Haanel)
- The Power of Self-Discipline (by Brian Tracey)
- Change Your Thoughts Change Your Life (by Dr. Wayne W. Dyer)
- Advice on Dying and Living A Better Life (by Dalai Lama)
- Secrets of The Millionaire Mind (by T. Harv Eker)
- Your Invisible Power (by Genevieve Behrend)
- The Hidden Power (by Thomas Troward)
- The Edinburgh Lectures On Mental Science (by Thomas Troward)

- The Power of Your Subconscious Mind (by Dr. Joseph Murphy)
- Rich Dad Poor Dad (by Robert Kiyosaki)
- As A Man Thinketh (by James Allen)
- The 5 AM Club (by Robin Sharma)
- The Wealth Mindset (by Neville Goddard)
- The Power of Your Awareness (Neville Goddard)
- The Gospel of Wealth (by Andrew Carnegie)

TIME IS NOT RUNNING OUT

BUT YOUR LIFE IS

× × × (CLAUDIA S.W) × × ×

Printed in Great Britain
by Amazon